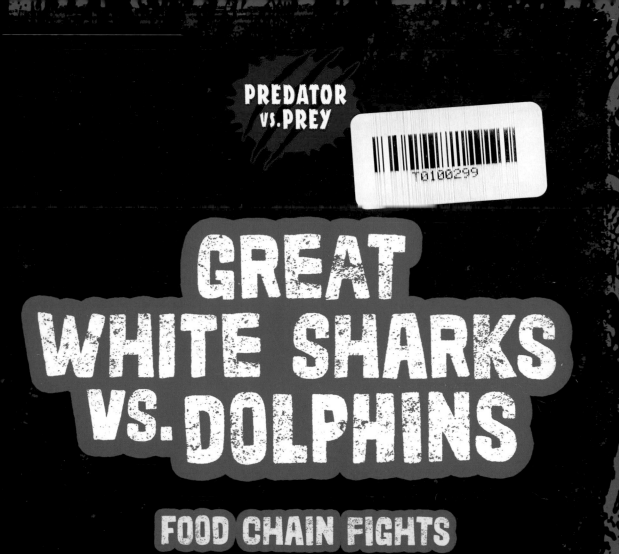

PREDATOR vs. PREY

GREAT WHITE SHARKS vs. DOLPHINS

FOOD CHAIN FIGHTS

BEN HUBBARD

Lerner Publications ◆ Minneapolis

For Agnieszka

Lerner Publications Company
An imprint of Lerner Publishing Group, Inc.
241 First Avenue North
Minneapolis, MN 55401 USA

For reading levels and more information, look up this title at www.lernerbooks.com.

Main body text set in Aptifer Sans LT Pro.
Typeface provided by Linotype AG.

Designer: Kim Morales

Library of Congress Cataloging-in-Publication Data

Names: Hubbard, Ben, 1973– author.
Title: Great white sharks vs. dolphins : food chain fights / Ben Hubbard.
Other titles: Great white sharks versus dolphins
Description: Minneapolis, MN : Lerner Publications, [2025] | Series: Predator vs. prey | Includes
   bibliographical references and index. | Audience: Ages 8–11 | Audience: Grades 4–6 | Summary:
   "Great white sharks and dolphins face off! Readers discover their size, speed, and more. They learn
   the strengths and weaknesses of this predator and prey pair. Then they uncover who would win in a
   fight"— Provided by publisher.
Identifiers: LCCN 2023038147 (print) | LCCN 2023038148 (ebook) | ISBN 9798765626740 (library
   binding) | ISBN 9798765629376 (paperback) | ISBN 9798765636169 (epub)
Subjects: LCSH: White shark—Juvenile literature. | Dolphins—Juvenile literature.
Classification: LCC QL638.95.L3 H83 2025 (print) | LCC QL638.95.L3 (ebook) | DDC 597.3/3—dc23/
   eng/20231102

LC record available at https://lccn.loc.gov/2023038147
LC ebook record available at https://lccn.loc.gov/2023038148

Manufactured in the United States of America
1-1010121-52005-12/4/2023

TABLE OF CONTENTS

CHAPTER 1
STRAY PREY IN THE SURF

IN THE PACIFIC OCEAN, A POD OF TWELVE DOLPHINS SPEEDS THROUGH THE WATER. The dolphins dive down and somersault into the air. As they play, they protect one another. They look out for predators. But one dolphin didn't keep up with the pod. The lone dolphin makes a clicking sound in the water. The sound bounces back to the dolphin. The echo tells the dolphin that no predators are in front of it. But something large is near its tail.

A dark shadow swims silently behind the dolphin. It is a great white shark. The shark is hungry and wants to make the dolphin its next meal. The shark dives deep and prepares to attack. It opens its mouth wide to reveal rows of razor-sharp teeth. The shark is about to strike!

A pod of dolphins

Will the shark get its meal? Will the dolphin escape to its pod? Each animal is about to fight for its life. But which one has the best tools to win the battle—predator or prey?

The great white shark is a skilled hunter. The shark uses stealth, strength, and speed to kill sea creatures. Its prey includes dolphins. The great white lives in most seas and oceans worldwide.

The bottlenose dolphin is one of the ocean's smartest creatures. It lives mainly in warm seas and oceans. It is both a predator and prey. Dolphins hunt together in a group. But they are hunted by tiger sharks, bull sharks, and great white sharks.

Great white sharks and bottlenose dolphins are both armed for battle. But which animal would win in a fight? Let's find out!

Great white sharks can live in cold waters but often live in warmer waters.

GREAT WHITE SHARK STATS

WEIGHT: 1,500 to 5,000 pounds (680 to 2,268 kg)

LENGTH: 11 to 21 feet (3.4 to 6.4 m)

TOP SWIMMING SPEED: 37 miles (60 km) per hour

BOTTLENOSE DOLPHIN STATS

WEIGHT: 300 to 1,400 pounds (136 to 635 kg)

LENGTH: 6.6 to 13.5 feet (2 to 4.1 m)

TOP SWIMMING SPEED: 22 miles (35 km) per hour

CHAPTER 2
GREAT WHITE SHARK VS. BOTTLENOSE DOLPHIN

GREAT WHITE SHARKS AND BOTTLENOSE DOLPHINS ARE BOTH TOUGH FIGHTERS. They have special features including: size, senses, and speed. Let's learn more about who is the ruler of the ocean habitat.

SIZE

The great white shark is the largest hunting fish on Earth. It has a bulky body shaped like a torpedo. Its shape makes the shark strong and fast. Great whites can take on the ocean's biggest prey: seals, dolphins, and whales.

The bottlenose dolphin is smaller than the great white shark. But it is powerful, with a strong tail and sleek body. This makes it fast and agile in the water. It is hard to catch and kill a dolphin.

A great white shark is about the size of three adult humans.

SENSES

Great white sharks use their senses to hunt. They have amazing eyesight, hearing, taste, and smell. They can smell blood in the water 1,640 feet (500 m) away. Great whites also have electroreception. This special sense lets them find electrical fields. Anytime an animal moves, it creates an electrical field. Electroreception helps sharks find prey, even when they are hidden in sand.

A great white shark opens its mouth before attacking its prey.

HOT OR COLD BLOOD?

Great white sharks can live in all water temperatures because they are warm-blooded. Most other sharks are cold-blooded.

Dolphins protect one another.

DOLPHINS CARE

Bottlenose dolphins are caring creatures. If one dolphin is hurt and can't surface, the others will help it to the surface to breathe.

Bottlenose dolphins are smart, social creatures. They communicate using squeaks, whistles, and clicks. They also use clicks to find other animals. They click into the water, and then the clicks return as echoes. This tells them if a predator or prey is nearby. This special sense is called echolocation. But echolocation only works for things in front of the dolphins.

LONG-RANGE HUNTERS

Great whites travel thousands of miles every year to hunt and breed.

SPEED

Great white sharks are built for speed. Their powerful tails push them quickly through the water. They can sprint at a top speed of 35 miles (56 km) per hour. That's as fast as an electric scooter. But great whites are also long-distance swimmers. They cruise the deep oceans at around 3.4 miles (5.5 km) per hour. This helps them save their energy.

A great white shark's tail helps it move fast.

Bottlenose dolphins can swim up to 100 miles (160.9 km) each day.

A bottlenose dolphin's smooth skin and body shape help it speed through water. These dolphins can swim at 22 miles (35 km) per hour. That's as fast as an eastern gray squirrel running on land. But usually, dolphins swim at about 5 miles (8 km) per hour.

AGILITY

Great white sharks are fast, but not agile. Their stiff bodies cannot make tight turns. The sharks are best at making a sprint in a straight line. They speed up from deep water to strike prey near the surface. Sometimes they even leap into the air. This is called breaching.

A shark breaches

CONFUSING COLORS

A great white's coloring helps it stay hidden. Its white belly looks like the sea's surface from below. From above, the shark's gray back looks like the dark seafloor.

BEST BOTTLENOSE BUDDIES

Bottlenose dolphins form friendships that can last for decades. They recognize one another by their individual clicks and whistles.

Bottlenose dolphins can leap as high as 20 feet (6 m) into the air.

Bottlenose dolphins are more agile than great whites. They have horizontal tails to make tight turns in the water. They can also breach the surface. No one is sure why dolphins breach. It may be to play or communicate with other dolphins.

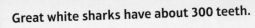

Great white sharks have about 300 teeth.

KEY WEAPONS

A great white shark uses its powerful jaws to strike. Its rows of razor-sharp teeth bite down on prey to help catch it. It then shakes its head from side to side to tear off chunks of flesh. It swallows the pieces whole.

A bottlenose dolphin's key weapons are its hard head and snout. It uses these weapons to ram into predators. A dolphin targets a predator's soft parts, such as its belly and gills. Together, dolphins can kill a creature with these ramming weapons.

Bottlenose dolphins get their name from their long snout.

HUNTING HABITS

Great white sharks hunt on their own. They prowl the deep ocean and coastal shores for food. They often visit places where prey lives in large numbers including seal colonies. Despite their size, great whites can hunt in waters as shallow as 15 feet (4.6 m) deep.

Great whites sometimes go to the surface when hunting.

Bottlenose dolphins are pack hunters. They swim together around a school of fish in tight circles. Then they pick off the fish with their sharp teeth. There are usually too many fish to catch them all. Dolphins also use their snouts to dig up and eat creatures from the sandy seafloor.

A dolphin catches a fish

TAIL FISH FLIPPER

Bottlenose dolphins use their tails to flip fish out of the water. They grab the stunned fish in their mouths.

ATTACKS AND DEFENSES

Great white sharks are ambush hunters. They hide in dark waters and sneak up on their prey. Sharks have trouble seeing. They bite what they are hunting to see if it is food. If it is prey, they will continue to attack. They will let go if it is not tasty. Great whites have a few predators, such as orcas. The shark's best defense is to avoid them. An orca will sometimes flip a great white on its back. This can stun it so it can't swim away.

A great white attacks a seal.

LEFTOVER EATERS

Great whites are scavengers as well as hunters. They will feed on dead creatures rotting in the water, such as whales.

Bottlenose dolphins have about 72 to 104 teeth.

Dolphins work together to defend themselves. They surround an attacking predator. Then they take turns ramming with their heads and snouts. They attack their own prey using their small, cone-shaped teeth. They grab prey such as fish with their teeth and can swallow some whole.

WEAKNESSES

Great white sharks can't move backward. They must keep moving forward to breathe through their gills. If a great white misses its prey, it has to swim around in a circle to attack again. This can give prey time to escape or attack. Great whites have weak areas around their gills, eyes, and bellies.

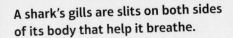

A shark's gills are slits on both sides of its body that help it breathe.

BREATHING AND BLOWING

Bottlenose dolphins are mammals. They need oxygen. They rise to the surface to breathe through their blowholes.

Dolphins' peduncles help them swim up and down.

Bottlenose dolphins have a weak area near their tail. This is the peduncle. It contains the dolphin's strongest muscles. It cannot swim without it. Great whites might bite the peduncle when hunting the dolphin.

CHAPTER 3
RULER OF THE HABITAT

FROM DEEP IN THE WATER, THE GREAT WHITE SHARK SPEEDS UP AND STRIKES THE BOTTLENOSE DOLPHIN. It hits so hard that both animals breach the water. The dolphin lies stunned near the surface. The shark makes a large turn to attack again. Whistling, squeaking, and clicking, the dolphin calls out to its pod. It needs help fast!

The great white gets ready to attack again. But then, a hard dolphin snout slams into the shark's gills. The pod has come to the rescue!

Dolphins race through waves.

The dolphins take turns ramming the shark. It has no choice but to swim away. Two dolphins then help the injured animal to the surface to breathe. Slowly, the dolphin starts to breathe again. It has survived the attack!

Great white sharks and bottlenose dolphins are both tough fighters. The great white is one of the ocean's fiercest predators. It lives to hunt and eat large prey. It has few predators.

But bottlenose dolphins can defend against a great white shark. Dolphins can speed away from an attack. But their best

Dolphins are safer when they stay together.

Great whites need to eat to live. If they don't get their prey, they have to find different prey to attack.

defense is staying in a group. Sharks rarely attack a whole pod of dolphins.

In this fight, the dolphin was the winner of the ocean habitat. The bottlenose dolphin survived the great white attack. But tomorrow it could be a different story. Maybe the great white will claim its prize. Predator and prey face off every day for their own survival.

PREDATOR VS. PREY: HEAD-TO-HEAD

DOLPHIN
- Streamlined body for speedy swimming
- Hard-ramming nose and head to attack

SHARK

- Rows of razor-sharp teeth to tear flesh
- Light and dark coloring provide camouflage

GLOSSARY

agile: able to move quickly and easily

blowhole: a nostril on the top of the head that some sea creatures breathe through

colony: a place where animals meet to breed and have babies

electrical field: a current of electricity made when an animal moves

habitat: the home of an animal or plant

mammal: a warm-blooded animal that feeds its young with milk made by the mother

predator: an animal that hunts and kills other animals for food

prey: an animal that is hunted and killed for food by a predator

school: a group of fish that swims together

sense: the ways an animal understands its surroundings. Some senses include touch, smell, taste, sight, and hearing

stealth: sneaking up on something without being seen

stun: to cause someone or something to suddenly become very confused

LEARN MORE

Britannica Kids: White Shark
https://kids.britannica.com/kids/article/great-white-shark/602043

Grodzicki, Jenna. *Pink River Dolphin*. Minneapolis: Bearport, 2023.

Markle, Sandra. *On the Hunt with Great White Sharks* Minneapolis: Lerner Publications, 2023.

Murray, Julie. *Great White Sharks*. Minneapolis: Cody Koala, 2024.

National Geographic Kids: Bottlenose Dolphin
https://kids.nationalgeographic.com/animals/mammals/facts/bottlenose -dolphin

National Geographic Kids: Great White Shark
https://kids.nationalgeographic.com/animals/fish/facts/great-white-shark

INDEX

PHOTO ACKNOWLEDGMENTS

Image credits: Blue Planet Archive/Doug Perrine, pp. 4, 5, 7; Carlos Villoch - MagicSea.com/Alamy, p. 6; WaterFrame/Alamy, pp. 7, 8, 9; Blue Planet Archive/Phillip Colla, p. 10; Blue Planet Archive/Jasmine Rossi, p. 11; AlexRoseShoots/Shutterstock, p. 12; Cultura Creative RF/Alamy, p. 13; MogensTrolle/Getty Images, p. 14; Mike Hill/Getty Images, p. 15; Harry Stone/Alamy, p. 16; Blue Planet Archive/Andre Seale, p. 17; Chris & Monique Fallows/Nature Picture Library/Alamy, pp. 18, 20; John Russell/Alamy, p. 19; Stephen Frink/Getty Images, p. 21; wildestanimal/Shutterstock, p. 22; Gerard Soury/Getty Images, p. 23; Blue Planet Archive/Michael S. Nolan, pp. 24, 25; Joost van Uffelen/Shutterstock, p. 26; Blue Planet Archive/David B. Fleetham, p. 27; Blue Planet Archive/Jeff Mondragon, p. 28; Wildestanimal/Alamy, p. 29. Design elements: iunewind/Shutterstock, Milano M/Shutterstock, Ukrainian studio/Shutterstock, Cassel/Shutterstock, Textures and backgrounds/Shutterstock, Print Net/Shutterstock.

Cover: Cat Gennaro/Getty Images, PacoRomero/Getty Images.